BODY MAGIC

The human body is probably the most wonderful and intricate of all creations – no man-made machine is half as efficient. Yet we who rely on it are often extremely ignorant of its uses, its functions and its possibilities.

BODY MAGIC is a collection of amazing stunts, tricks and activities designed to help you get to know your body. You can have a lot of fun trying, for example, the optical illusions which show how the eyes and brain function, attempting balancing skills and experimenting with tests of touch. And you will learn some pretty extraordinary facts – did you know, for instance, that a piece of skin the size of a 5p coin contains over three million cells, 100 sweat glands and 25 nerve endings? Read on and discover a whole lot more amazing facts with which to stun your friends . . .

Also in Beaver by Peter Eldin

How to be a Detective

Peter Eldin

BODY MAGIC

Cartoons by Terry Riley

Beaver Books

A Beaver Original

Published by Arrow Books Limited
17–21 Conway Street, London W 1P 6JD

A division of the Hutchinson Publishing Group

London Melbourne Sydney Auckland
Johannesburg and agencies throughout the world

First published 1984

©Copyright text Eldin Editorial Services 1984
©Copyright text diagrams the Hutchinson Publishing Group 1984
©Copyright cartoons the Hutchinson Publishing Group 1984

Set in Linoterm Bembo by JH Graphics

Made and printed in Great Britain
by the Anchor Press Ltd
Tiptree, Essex

ISBN 09 938 070 6

Contents

1 Before Your Very Eyes   7
2 You Need Hands   19
3 Tricks of Co–ordination and Balance   34
4 Tests of Strength   43
5 Body Stunts and Tricks   54
6 Play the Game   65

1   Before Your Very Eyes

Sight is our most important sense but it is amazing how easily your senses can be tricked. Try these stunts on yourself and your friends and you will see what I mean.

Making the Invisible Visible

Look at the picture on this page. Can you see a white triangle with each corner resting on a black circle?

Although you can see it the triangle does not exist. Take a closer look and you will realize that the white triangle has not been drawn at all. It is simply your brain that has imagined it!

If you do not believe this, draw the picture for yourself. As you draw in the black circles the white triangle will appear as if by magic.

Amazing Arrows

Look at the two arrows on this page.

It is obvious that the top one is longer than the bottom one.

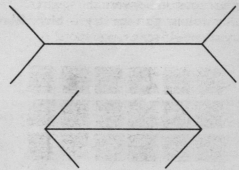

Or is it?

Get a ruler and measure them both. You will find that they are both exactly the same length.

Which Way?

In which direction are these triangles pointing?

Up, down, to the right, or to the left?

One minute they appear to be pointing upwards but as you watch they seem to change their direction— and the more you watch, the more they seem to move!

Spots Before the Eyes

Look at the black squares on this page for a minute or so.

After a while you should start to see dark spots at the places where the white lines meet.

Having tried that, draw the squares in the same pattern on a sheet of paper but colour them red. If you look at this pattern for a while you should start to see green spots in between the squares.

Another colour you can try is blue. With blue squares you should see orange spots!

Line Up

Here is a well-known optical illusion. Look at the picture on this page and see if you can guess whether AC is a straight line or if BC is a straight line.

Most people would think that AC is the straight line. It certainly looks like it.

But if you put a ruler on the line you will see that C is really the other end of the line that starts at B.

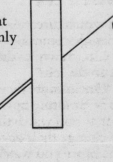

Going Round in Circles

Hold this book in one hand, and move your hand in a horizontal circular motion as you look at the circles on this page. It seems as though the circles are moving of their own accord.

How moving!

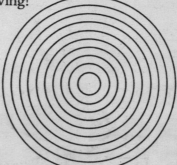

What Does It Say?

Take a quick look at this sign. What does it say?

If you think it says 'PARIS IN THE SPRING' take another look. It really says 'PARIS IN THE THE SPRING'.

Show it to your family and friends. You will find that most people will get it wrong.

BODY FACT

Don't worry if someone says you have got water on the brain. They are right – for the human brain is 80 per cent water.

High Hat

If you look at the hat worn by the gentleman on this page you could be forgiven for thinking that its height is greater than the width of its brim. It certainly looks that way, doesn't it?

But if you measure both the height and the width you will find that they are exactly the same. Yes, your brain has tricked you once again!

Topsy Turvy Steps

Take a look at the flight of steps on this page. They appear quite ordinary, but if you keep looking at them for a while a strange thing will happen. They will turn themselves upside down!

At first it appears that you are looking down on the steps and then, just a few seconds later, it seems that you are underneath the steps and looking up at them from below.

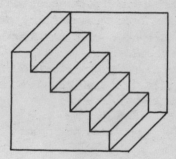

The Tumbling Cube

Look at this cube for a while and it seems to turn itself over. You seem to be looking down on it one minute and up at it the next just like the steps in the picture above.

Strange, isn't it!

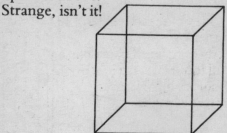

A Piece of Cake

Who likes cake? You do? Well then, you might like to look at the picture on this page.

Apart from the fact that someone has taken a slice from the cake it looks fairly ordinary, doesn't it?

But turn the page upside down and something very strange happens.

It now appears that the cake is in a dish and there is only one slice left. Someone must have eaten the rest when you weren't looking!

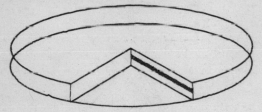

Paper Perplexer

From a sheet of paper cut out three strips each of the same length. One of the strips should be half the width of the other two.

Lay out the three strips of paper like this and they all look the same length. This is hardly surprising because they *are* all the same length.

Rearrange the strips into this formation:

As you can see, it looks as if the narrow strip is shorter than the other two.

Rearrange the strips again and put them down like this:

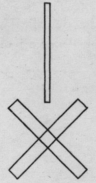

It now looks as if the narrow strip is much longer than the other two. How peculiar!

BODY FACT

During the average lifetime the human heart pumps 300,000 tons of blood around your body.

Pin–Hole Pin

Make a small pin-hole in the centre of a piece of card or stiff paper.

Hold the card in front of a bright light and about 15–20cm from one eye. Close your other eye. Focus your open eye (and your attention!) on the hole. Now hold the pin between the card and your eye so that the pin head comes in line with the hole.

You may have to move the pin a little until you get it in the correct position but eventually you should be able to see a shadowy image of the pin. But – surprise, surprise – the pin is seen upside down!

Keep your gaze on the hole and do not focus on the pin when doing this or it will not work.

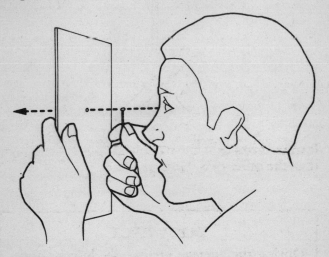

When you finish this experiment, do not throw the pin and card away. You can use them for the next experiment.

Double It

Take the piece of card you used for *Pin-hole pin*, and make another pin–hole close to the first. The two holes should not be more than 3mm apart.

With one eye (close the other) look through both of the holes at the same time. hold the pin on the far side of the card about 2–3cm away. You should now see two pins!

If you go one step further and make a third hole in the card so that the three holes form a triangle you will be able to see three pins when you look through the holes.

Multiplying Money

Place two coins of the same value on the table in front of you. The coins should be about 3–5cm apart.

Now hold a pencil between the two coins.

Focus your eyes on the tip of the pencil and gradually bring the pencil up towards your face. If you keep your gaze focused on the pencil the coins will appear to merge into one.

Continue to bring the pencil nearer to your face. It gets harder to keep your eyes focused on the pencil point as it gets closer to your face, but if you do you will eventually see the 'single' coin split into four!

Sounds like an easy way to get rich quick!

FLOUR POWER

Have you noticed that your mouth dries up when you are nervous? This fact was used as a test of guilt in the Middle Ages. Suspects had to put flour in their mouths, the idea being that guilty people would be so nervous that their mouths would dry up and they would be unable to swallow the flour. The people who were innocent would not be quite so apprehensive (in theory!) and so their glands would produce enough saliva to enable them to swallow the flour easily.

Seeing Red

No doubt you have heard the old joke: What is black and white and red all over? Answer: A newspaper (red = read!).

Here is a way you can make that joke come true.

Draw a large circle on a piece of card and colour one half of it black.

Cut the circle out and also cut a wedge from it so it looks like this:

Push a knitting needle or a pencil through the centre of the disc. Place the point of the needle or pencil on a newspaper and position the disc so it is about 5 cm above the paper.

If you now spin the disc you will be surprised to find that the newsprint, when viewed through the gap in the disc, appears to be red. (Or should that be 'read'?)

BODY FACT

In an average lifetime a human breathes 500 million times.

---

2 You Need Hands

Human hands are very versatile. They can do lots of different things. They can even be used to do tricks and stunts like the ones in this chapter. Handy that!

Wing, Wing, Wing

Ask a friend to close one hand into a fist and rest his other hand on top of it.

Now ask him to say 'wing' three times.

He says: 'Wing, wing, wing.' You now pick up his hand as if it was a telephone, place it to your ear, and say 'Hello'.

Sounds crazy – but it will make your other friends laugh like mad.

BODY FACT

There are about two million pores, or sweat glands, scattered over the whole surface of your skin. On the palms of your hands there are about 3000 pores in every square inch of skin.

The skin normally pours out well over a pint of perspiration each day. Someone exercising in very hot weather could easily lose up to three pints of perspiration an hour.

Hot and Cold

For this experiment you will need three bowls of water – one hot, one cold, and one warm.

Place one hand in the cold water and one hand in the hot water (don't have it too hot!)

Keep the hands immersed for a minute or two, then put both hands into the warm water.

You will now experience a strange sensation. The water will feel both hot and cold at the same time!

Why?

Ask a friend if she can ask a question using just one finger.

When she gives up you show her how it is done.

Just bend your forefinger in half, down upon itself and you will see that the creases in the flesh form the letter 'Y'. And that is the question – Why?

Aristotle's Illusion

Cross the first and second fingers of one hand. Now use those fingers to feel a marble as shown in the illustration.

You will be surprised to find that you can feel two marbles! This is especially effective if you close your eyes so you cannot see there is really only one marble between your fingers.

This strange phenomenon is called 'Aristotle's Illusion' because it was first described by the Greek philosopher Aristotle over two thousand years ago.

The Missing Finger

Tell your friends that you have lost a finger. To prove it you show your hand with the second finger bent down as in the first picture.

Before your friends have time to say anything turn your hand over from the wrist to show the palm. At the same time you straighten out your second finger and immediately open your fingers to cause a gap between the second and third fingers as shown in the second picture.

Turn the hand palm down again. At the same time reverse the above movements so you are back to the first position once again.

Do these movements two or three times and it creates quite a realistic impression that the finger really is missing.

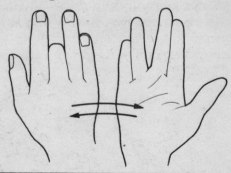

BODY FACT

The hardest working part of the body is undoubtedly the heart muscle. Each day, contracting at a rate of 70 to 75 times a minute, it pumps over 3000 gallons of blood around the body.

How To Be An Idiot

This really is quite silly, but it looks rather funny. So if you are the type who likes to make your friends laugh this stunt is ideal for you.

Form your left hand into a fist and hold it in front of you with the thumb on top. Now push the right forefinger up through the fist from below so it sticks out of the fist near the left thumb.

Wiggle the finger for a few seconds. Then quickly remove the right hand and try to grab the finger.

As the finger is no longer there (because it is attached to the right hand) this action looks absolutely crazy.

It looks even crazier if you repeat it a few times.

Threaded Fingers

Here is another crazy stunt you can do to amuse your friends.

Pretend to thread an imaginary needle with cotton.

Now mime the action of sewing the cotton to your left elbow.

You then pretend to push the needle through your little finger and back to the elbow.

Now thread each of the other fingers in the same way.

When you have finished threading all the fingers you take the imaginary thread at the elbow and pull it. As you pull you close the fingers of the left hand.

Relax the imaginary thread and your fingers open out again.

Do this several times as if working your fingers like a puppeteer pulling strings.

Your friends will think you are mad!

BODY FACT

Nine people out of ten are right-handed.

Thumb Fun

Ask a friend to place her right thumb into her palm, exactly as shown in the picture. With the thumb in this position she has then to bring her hand up so that the right fingers can touch underneath her right armpit.

Tell her to move her thumb out and away from the palm. This she will be able to do quite easily.

Now challenge her to put it
back into exactly the same
position.

She will find it just cannot be done. In fact she
may even find that it is quite painful to try this
apparently simple movement.

BODY FACT

Most of us suffer from hiccoughs from time to
time but it usually goes away after holding
one's breath, drinking upside down or trying
one of the many other recommended cures.
Jack O'Leary of Los Angeles, USA, could not
get rid of the problem so easily.

His ailment started on 13 June, 1948, and,
with the exception of one week in 1951,
continued unabated until 1 June, 1956.
Naturally he tried all of the popular cures and
60,000 suggestions advocated by fellow
sufferers but to no avail. Eventually one cure
was successful—a prayer to St Jude, the patron
saint of lost causes, did the trick and the
hiccoughing stopped. Even today Jack
O'Leary still holds the uncomfortable record
for the longest attack of hiccoughs on record.

The Dead Finger

Hold a friend's left hand with your right, inter-twining your fingers together. Now both of you extend the first finger so your hands look like this:

Ask your friend to run his right finger and thumb up and down the fingers so that his thumb is touching his own finger but his forefinger is touching your finger.

He will think his brain is playing tricks on him for he will discover that it feels as if his left forefinger is dead on one side.

It is quite an uncanny feeling.

BODY FACT

If you never cut your fingernails they could grow to over 2 metres long. But the longest fingernail on record was that of Romesh Sharma of Delhi in India which when measured in 1980 was 67cm long. It took 13 years to reach that length.

Crash!

Put your two fists together with the thumbs touching. Now ask someone to press his knuckles against your knuckles as shown in the illustration.

When he is pressing hard you quickly withdraw your hands and his fists will crash together. He may not like the idea of banging his fists together so be ready to run away fast!

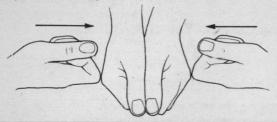

BODY FACT

The middle fingernail on each of your hands grows faster than any of your other fingernails.

The Power of Suggestion

Get some unsuspecting friend to clasp his hands together with the two index fingers outstretched as shown in the illustration.

Say that you are now going to exert the power of your supersonic brain against his feeble jelly of a brain and that you will make his fingers move together just by the power of your thoughts.

Wave your hands around his a few times, utter a few magic words (which you have just made up) and, much to his surprise (and to yours, too), his fingers gradually move together!

The power of suggestion has something to do with the success of this trick but mainly it is due to the fact that his fingers get tired in this position and automatically move towards each other.

BODY FACT

Your fingernails grow faster in warm weather than they do in cold weather.

The Broken Wrist

This stunt has no purpose whatsoever – but it is quite funny and it will convince all your mates that you are absolutely crazy.

Hold your left arm outstretched. With your right hand tap the inside of the elbow (at the point marked with an arrow in the picture 1). As you do this, whip the forearm up to the position shown in picture 2.

Now tap the back of your left hand and allow it to flop down to the position shown in picture 3.

For the last movement the right hand twists the left hand to the position shown in picture 4. Scream, or make a creaking noise, as you do this. Although people watching you may not really believe you have broken your wrist, many will think that it is a painful movement.

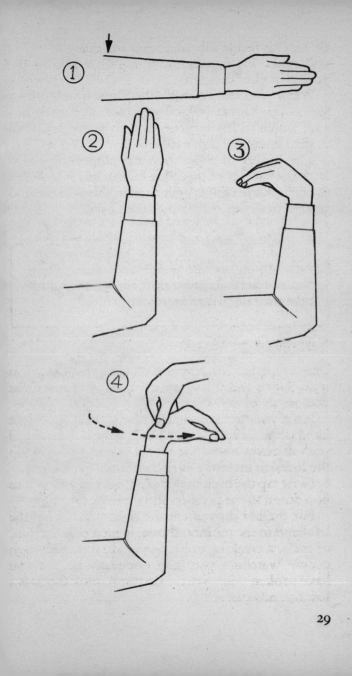

29

NATURAL BREAKS

Did you know that there are as many as 206 bones in the skeleton of an adult person? Younger people have more bones but as they get older some of them fuse together. The spinal column, for example, is originally made up of 33 separate bones, called *vertebrae*. In later life five of these bones join together to form one large bone, the *sacrum*. Another four vertebrae fuse together into the *coccyx*.

It used to be believed that bones were supple in warm weather and brittle in cold, but this is nothing but an old wives' tale. It probably came about because people are more likely to slip and break a bone during the winter months when ice and snow are on the ground.

Thumbs Up

Your friends will be absolutely amazed when you
calmly remove your thumb and then, just as calmly,
restore it to its original state. It looks horrifying, but
is in fact very easy to do.

Hold your left hand with its back facing your
audience. The right hand now takes hold of the left
thumb and moves it back and forth as if trying to
break it off.

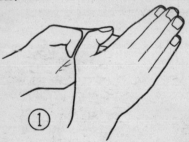

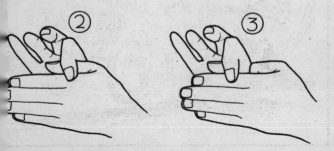

Remove the right hand for a moment as you inspect your left thumb. Now bring the right hand back to the left once again. This time, however, your right fingers conceal the left thumb momentarily.

As soon as the left thumb is hidden, bend it inwards at the knuckle. At the same time bend the right thumb and place it alongside the left thumb. Picture 1 shows the position of the thumbs at this stage. The other fingers have been moved out of the way to enable you to see the position clearly.

As soon as you have attained this position you can lift the right fingers with the exception of the forefinger. The right forefinger covers the join between the left and right thumbs. From the audience's point of view the hands now look like those shown in picture 2.

Now move the right hand to the right. It appears that part of the left thumb is being removed as shown in picture 3.

To restore the thumb all you have to do is to reverse the above moves and then separate the hands.

There are two important points to bear in mind to make this stunt more effective.

1. When 'removing' the thumb keep the right thumb in contact with the left forefinger.

2. Only show the stunt to people who are standing directly in front of you. People on either side will be able to see that the thumbs are bent.

BODY FACT

About two-thirds of the body of an adult person consists of water.

Long and Short

Hold your right hand up with the palm facing you. Now grasp the top of the little finger between the forefinger and thumb of the left hand.

Picture 1 shows your view and picture 2 is what your friends will see. Note that the left fingers hide all but the top of the right little finger from view.

Now pull the left hand down causing the right little finger to bend. At first your finger may resist this bending but try to relax it and after a while you will find it bends quite easily.

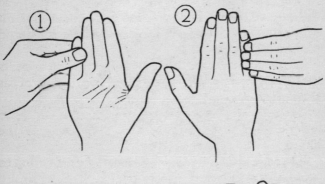

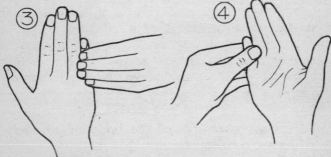

Because the left fingers conceal the bending of the little finger everyone watching will receive the impression that you have compressed the little finger as shown in picture 3. Picture 4 shows your view at this stage.

Move the left hand up and down a few times and it looks as if you can shorten and lengthen your little finger at will.

3   Tricks of Co-ordination and Balance

If we could not co-ordinate our movements we would not get much done. If we could not balance we would fall over! Try the stunts on the following pages and see how good your co-ordination is and see how often you and your friends fall over when trying some of the balancing stunts.

Finger Flexing

This is a test of co-ordination that you and your friends can try.

Hold out your left hand with a large gap between the second and third fingers. Place your right hand alongside it but with a gap between the first and second fingers.

Now see if you can change positions so that the gap on the left is between the first and second fingers and that on the right is between the second and third fingers.

When you have managed that, try going back to the original position.

Now repeat the movements.

Each hand should be changed at exactly the same time and as quickly as you can manage. It requires quite a lot of concentration and a fair deal of practice to get it right every time.

Russian Dance

You may have seen Russian dancers, or people imitating them, squat down on their haunches and then kick out their legs alternately. But have you ever tried to do it yourself? It looks easier than it really is. But it is worth trying – if only for a laugh. Who knows? You may even get good at it.

Squat down on your right heel with your left leg extended straight out in front of you.

Now all you have to do is to change the position of your legs. Stick out your right leg and, at the same time, bring your left leg in and below your body.

Do this several times and you will be dancing like a real Russian! It is, however, more than likely that you will just fall over!

BODY FACT

You are taller in the morning than you are at night.

Miner's Seat

This method of squatting was taught to me by a coal miner. He and his friends sat like this when they were underground.

Start from a standing position.

Now bend your knees until you are squatting. Your heels will be raised from the ground at this point, and this makes it a difficult position to maintain for any length of time.

The next step is to lower your heels to the

ground. When you try this for the first time you will probably find that you will fall backwards and end up with a sore bottom. The secret is to have your feet reasonably well apart and to lean forward slightly as you go down.

After a little bit of practice you will find that it is quite easy to adopt the position shown in the picture and that you can stay in this position for a long time without any strain. Handy if you happen to be working at a coal face.

The Talented Elephant

Ask your friends if they have ever seen an elephant do a 'handstand'. Some may have actually seen this at a circus or on television and they will tell you so.

You then say that you will show them your remarkable impression of an elephant doing a 'handstand'.

Squat down and place both your hands flat on the floor. Now position your knees outside your arms so that the inner part of each knee is in contact with one of your elbows.

All you now have to do is gradually move your head and upper body forward and lift your feet from the ground. It sounds impossible and it must be admitted that it is not easy to do at first. You may fall over several times until you get the knack.

When you succeed for the first time you will deserve a reward – so go down to the local river and treat yourself to a trunk full of water.

Pick It Up

See how good your balance is when you try this stunt.

Put a broomstick or a long pole behind your knees. Now put your arms behind the pole and place your hands on the ground in front of you.

Get someone to put a small object, such as a matchbox or a bunched-up handkerchief, on the ground in front of you.

Can you now pick up the object in your teeth without falling over?

The Mirror Test

For this experiment you will need a mirror, a pencil, some paper and a magazine.

Place the mirror so that it is upright. Put the paper on the table in front of the mirror. Now hold the magazine in one hand so that you can see the paper reflected in the mirror but in such a way that the paper itself is hidden from your sight.

Take the pencil and, using just the image in the mirror to guide you, draw a square. Although a little awkward to do you should be able to manage this fairly easily. Now try to draw diagonal lines from corner to corner of the square. That is not so easy – as you will discover when you try it.

Finger Roll

Hold both your hands out in front of you with the forefingers pointing at each other.

Now rotate the right forefinger so that its tip describes a circle. Easy, isn't it! Do the same with the left forefinger. That is easy as well.

Now comes the difficult bit.

Rotate both fingers at the same time – but in opposite directions.

That's not so easy, is it?

It's Yours!

Place a coin on the floor near to a wall. Get a friend to stand with his back to the wall and with both his head and his heels touching it.

Tell him that if he can now bend down and pick up the coin he can have it. There is just one rule – he is not allowed to move his feet forward or raise his heels from the floor.

Don't worry – your money will be absolutely safe. It just cannot be done!

Get It Write

Hand a friend a sheet of paper and a pencil and tell her that all you want her to do is write the word 'knowledge' on the paper.

There is just one little snag.

While your friend is writing she must describe a continuous circle, about the size of a dinner plate, with her right foot.

Try as she may she will find it almost impossible to write the word (any word will do) while her foot is in motion. If she does manage to start writing reasonably well she has probably also changed the movement of her foot.

Like most co–ordination stunts, this one can be done with practice. So after several of your friends have tried and failed you can show them how easy it is. They will not know that you have been prac-tising in secret.

BODY FACT

Most people have legs of slightly different lengths – usually the left leg is slightly shorter than the right leg.

Get Them Together

Stand with your feet apart, so that your left foot and your left shoulder are touching a wall.

Now all you have to do is to put your feet together without moving your left foot and shoulder from the wall.

Sounds easy, doesn't it?

But just try it for yourself and you will find it is not as simple as it sounds.

Stool Stand

Get a stool and place it alongside a wall. Now stand facing the stool. You should be at least 30 cm away from the stool.

Bend over until you can grasp the seat of the stool between both hands. Your head should be pressed against the wall.

Lift the stool from the ground.

That was easy, wasn't it?

But that is not the task you have to undertake!

You now have to stand up straight, still holding the stool.

That is not so easy. In fact it is absolutely impossible and you are now stuck in this position!

The only way to get out of your predicament is to replace the stool on the floor and use it as a support to enable you to regain an upright position!

4 Tests of Strength

Want to prove you are tougher than your mates? This section shows you how. Many of these stunts were performed in theatres towards the end of the last century by Lulu Hurst, the Georgia Wonder; and Annie Abbot, the Little Georgia Magnet to prove they were stronger than the toughest of men. You can do the same.

Impossible Lift

This is one of the spectacular stunts performed by Lulu Hurst and Annie Abbot. It is especially effective if you use someone who is obviously bigger and stronger than you are.

First you ask your volunteer to lift you. This he does quite easily – as everyone will expect, especially if you are quite small compared to your assistant.

Now you say that you will exert your immense mental power so that your friend will become as weak as a kitten so he will not be able to lift you any longer. Much to his surprise, no matter how much effort he exerts he is now unable to lift you off the ground.

Those of you who are scientifically minded may wish to know that this feat has got absolutely nothing to do with the strength or weakness of your volunteer. It is accomplished by the fact that you alter your centre of balance to make the lift impossible. You do this in a crafty, and unseen manner.

For the first lift fold your arms up to your chest so your elbows are pointing directly towards the ground. The person who lifts you is asked to face you and then place one hand beneath each of your elbows. Provided that your volunteer is reasonably strong he should have little difficulty in getting you off the ground.

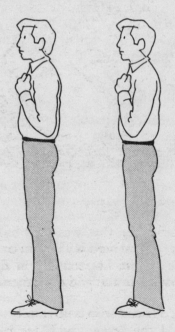

To everyone watching the next attempt appears to be exactly the same. In fact you have moved your elbows forward slightly. This small change of position is enough to alter your centre of balance to such a degree that the lifter is no longer able to get you off the ground.

To make it even more difficult for him, hold your arms and shoulders loosely when he tries to lift you.

A Test of Strength

This is another test that was used by Lulu Hurst. Once again, all you need is a broom or a long pole.

Hold the broom horizontally in front of you. Use both hands for this and place them about 30cm apart.

Now ask a friend who is obviously stronger than you to hold the broom with his hands outside yours, as shown in the picture on the next page.

Your friend has now to pit his strength against yours and try to push you off balance. He must give a steady push and he is not allowed to pull the broom towards him at all to give him an unfair advantage. No matter how hard he tries he is unable to get you off balance.

The secret of this stunt is not to push back against your stronger friend but to push upwards slightly. This forces your opponent to try to keep the broom level so she is unable to exert her full strength against you.

Pull Them Apart

With this stunt any weedy weakling can prove he is stronger than the strongest bully. You can challenge the school bully to this and no matter how strong he is he will not be able to succeed.

Lift your elbows up to the level of your shoulders and touch the tips of your forefingers together as shown in the illustration.

Now challenge the strongest person you know to pull your fingers apart. To do this he must stand facing you and grasp your wrists. He must give a steady pull and is not allowed to put you off balance by any sudden jerks.

No matter how strong he is nor how hard he tries he will not be able to do it – unless of course you are the weakest weakling of all time.

BODY FACT

There are about 650 muscles in your body. They vary in length from less than 25cm to over a half a metre.

Push Hard

This is a good way to 'prove' that your strength as an individual is greater than the combined strength of up to ten other people.

Face a wall and place your palms flat against it with your fingers pointing upwards. Your arms should be straight.

Now ask several people to stand in a line behind you. Each person should stretch out his or her arms and place his or her hands on the shoulders of the person in front.

Ask everyone to push as hard as they can so that you will be flattened against the wall.

Don't worry. You will not end up as a human pancake!

As long as you can resist the strength of the person immediately behind you there is nothing to worry about.

Each person in the line is absorbing the efforts of the person behind him or her so you have only the strength of one person to contend with.

Poles Apart

For this test of strength you will need two long poles, or brooms, and at least ten metres of rope.

Get the four strongest people you know each to hold one end of a pole horizontally at arm's length.

Now tie one end of the rope to the end of one of the poles. Wind the rest of the rope around the poles as shown in the picture. Make sure that the rope does not cross itself at any point.

Take the free end of the rope and challenge your friends to try to keep the poles apart as you pull on the rope.

No matter how much of a weakling you may be you will find it a fairly easy matter to get the poles together by pulling on your end of the rope.

Hold It!

This is something that just cannot be done. No even the strongest person in the world can do it And yet it sounds very easy.

All you have to do is balance a glass tumbler o your hand for just seven minutes, keeping your arm outstretched all the time.

Try it. You will find that it is impossible – so wil all your mates.

There's No Escape

Tell a friend that you can get him to hold his hand together in such a way that he will not be able to leave the room without unclasping them.

This sounds impossible so he is very likely to call your bluff and challenge you to do it.

You then get him to clasp his hands around the leg of a piano, a table or anything else that he cannot move out of the room. He cannot now leave the room without unclasping his hands.

BODY FACT

About 43 muscles are used to cause a frown but only about 15 muscles are needed to raise a smile. So smile – it is less tiring!

Time For a Break

Ask a friend if she is strong enough to break a match. She will probably snort in disgust (or whatever your friends do when they are upset) and angrily reply that of course she can break it.

You now spring your trap for you show her an ordinary wooden match. Lay it across the back of her middle finger, near the nail, and underneath her first and third fingers. She has now to keep her hand and fingers perfectly straight and try to break the match by pushing down with the first and third fingers and up with the second finger.

Only a few people can actually manage to break the match in this position.

Fingers Against Fists

Ask the strongest person you know to hold his closed fists together, one on top of the other. He is to press them together as tightly as he can.

If you now hit each fist with your fingertips on either side you can separate the fists quite easily. Because your friend is concentrating on keeping the fists together by downward pressure from the top fist and upward pressure from the bottom fist it is an easy matter for you to knock them sideways.

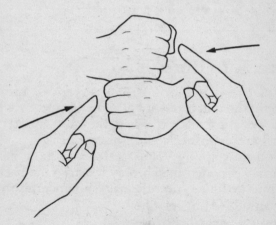

Give Someone the Brush Off

For this body trick you will need a household broom. If you do not have a broom handy a billiard cue or a long stick will do just as well.

Ask someone to hold the broom in a vertical position between his hands, one hand being near the top of the broom handle and the other near to the bottom.

All you do is place the palm of your right hand (assuming that you are right-handed) against the broom handle as shown in the picture.

Your friend has now to try to force the broom handle down until it touches the floor.

All you have to do is press hard enough against the handle to make sure that you do not lose contact with it.

This is enough to deflect the other person's energy and no matter how hard he tries he will never get the broom handle to touch the floor.

5 Body Stunts and Tricks

In this section you will find all sorts of unusual things you can do with your body. Try them out – they are all great fun.

Soft Shoe Shuffle

This does not serve any useful purpose but it was once very popular with comedians. In recent years it has become one of the movements used by dancers who do robotics (moving like a robot). Basically it is a way of moving from one place to another without actually walking.

This is how you do a soft shoe shuffle. It sounds difficult, but once you get going, and get some speed up, it is quite simple.

1. Stand with your feet slightly apart.
2. Rise up on the balls of your feet and move both heels to the left.
3. Lean back on to your heels and then swivel your toes to the left.
4. Repeat move 2.
5. Repeat move 3.

Keep repeating these movements and you will get from one place to another.

Charleston Knees

Many years ago there was a dance called 'The
Charleston'. In one version of the dance there was a
funny movement that is worth knowing if you
want the reputation of being a comedian – or an
idiot!

Bend down slightly and rest your right hand on
your right knee and your left hand on your left knee.
Bring your knees together and as they touch
continue to move your right hand to the left and
your left hand to the right as the knees open out once
again. In other words, your right hand transfers to
your left knee and your left hand moves over to
your right knee.

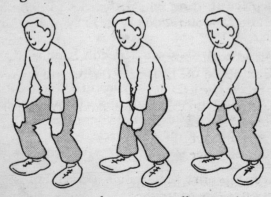

As soon as your knees are well apart they move
back together again. At this point your right hand is

55

moved back to your right knee and your left hand moves back to the left knee.

Sounds complicated, doesn't it!

It is not really difficult. Just take it slowly to begin with and you should be able to do it fairly easily. Keep repeating the movements and your friends will think it looks very funny (or they will decide that you are absolutely crazy).

BODY FACT

The famous Italian artist, scientist, and mathematician Leonardo da Vinci once described the human foot as the greatest engineering device in the world.

Male or Female?

Get a piece of string about half a metre in length. To one end of the string tie a ring, a key or anything of similar weight.

Hold the string over a friend's hand so that the ring is about 3–5cm from the palm.

Keep the string as still as you can and concentrate.

If your friend is a boy the ring will swing back and forth in a straight line. But if your friend is a girl the ring will move around in a circle.

Try it and you will find that it really does work in most cases.

Although you are trying to keep the string steady you are actually moving it through minute movements in your fingers.

BODY FACT

The average man has about 20 square feet of skin and the average woman about 17 square feet. The whole skin weighs about five pounds and is the largest organ in the body.

Human skin varies in thickness from about ½ mm on the lips to about 6 mm on the soles of the feet.

It's A Draw

Ask a friend to draw any simple geometrical figure, such as a square, circle or triangle, with another simple shape inside it. He or she must not let you see what has been drawn.

You now take another piece of paper and draw the figure shown on this page. Ask your friend to turn over his or her piece of paper as you show yours.

It does not work every time but you have a good chance that your drawings will match. If only one of the two figures is right tell your friend off for not concentrating hard enough.

You may find that this trick works better if you get an adult to draw the pictures.

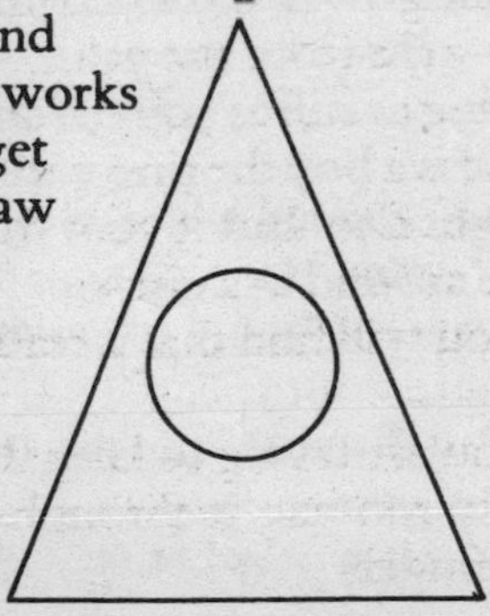

Untouchable

Can you put your right hand where your left hand cannot reach it?

You can if you place your right hand on your left elbow. Your left hand certainly cannot reach it there.

Now try it on your friends.

I've Got Your Number

Write the numbers 1 to 9 in a circle as shown here:

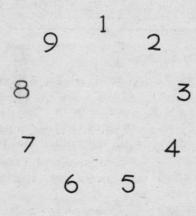

Hand a friend a pencil and ask him to cross out any number. Meanwhile, take paper and pencil yourself and write the figure 9 on the paper. Fold it over and hand it to your friend.

Most people will cross out the 9. Like the last experiment, this does not work every time. And you may find that it works better with adults.

Ask your friend to open the piece of paper you have given him, and keep your fingers crossed that he has crossed out the number 9 on the circle!

You can make this stunt more convincing if you get a number of people to do it all at the same time. With a bit of luck you will have several people cross out the 9.

The numbers need not be in the order shown here. In fact it makes no difference what the numbers are, for people will still pick the one to the left of the top number.

BODY FACT

You are more liable to sneeze if your feet are cold.

Weighty Coins

For this stunt you need three identical coins.

Put one in the fridge – yes, that's right, in the fridge!

You do an even stranger thing with the other two coins – you put them into a warm oven!

When the single coin is cold and the other two coins are warm you can try this experiment with a friend.

Ask a friend to lie down on her back. Now place the cold coin on her forehead. Ask her to think about the weight of the coin.

After a short while take the coin away and replace it with the two warm coins.

When you ask your friend about the weight this time you will find that she thinks it is no more than that of the single coin.

What Shape?

From a sheet of card cut out two long, thin strips.

Use one strip to make a square and another to make a triangle like the ones shown. Each figure should be roughly the same size.

Now blindfold a friend and press one of the shapes against his forearm. Unless the shapes are very large he will not be able to distinguish one from the other.

Try the same experiment on the palm of his hand and he will know instantly which is which. The palm is more sensitive than the forearm so even if the shapes are made extremely small they can still be told apart.

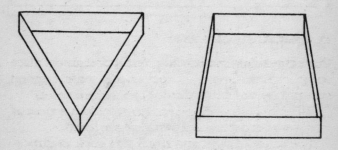

BODY FACT

Shivering is the body's way of warming itself up in cold conditions. When the muscles shiver they generate heat in the blood. Some muscles, such as those of the fingers and feet, have little blood in them so they are more susceptible to the cold.

Brush Up

Show your friend a clothes brush and begin to brush the back of his coat. At least, that is what he thinks you are doing. What you really do is stroke his back with your free hand and at the same time use the brush to brush your own coat!

Provided that you move both hands at the same time your friend will believe that you are really brushing his coat. This should give your other friends who are watching quite a laugh.

BODY FACT

As a general rule women live longer than men.

A Question of Taste

Place three saucers on a table. In the first saucer place some crushed apple, in the second some crushed raw potato and in the third some crushed onion.

Blindfold a friend and get her to hold her nose as you give her a spoonful of one of the foods.

The sense of sight and smell play such an important part in the way we taste food that she will not be able to tell which food is which when deprived of these senses.

BODY FACT

A piece of human skin about the size of a 5p piece contains a metre of blood vessels, about 25 nerve endings, 100 sweat glands, and over a million cells!

Stuck

If you can persuade a friend to fall for this you and your other friends will have a good laugh.

Ask your friend to wrap his legs around a lamp-post or a smooth tree, so that he takes up the position shown in the illustration.

Now ask him to slide down the pole until he is sitting on the ground.

You and your friends can now walk away and your poor hapless victim will be stuck. It is very difficult to get up from the position you have just put him in.

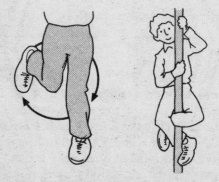

BODY FACT

During a lifetime the average person eats about 35 tons of food. That is equivalent to the weight of five African elephants!

Going Up

Stand in an open doorway and press the backs of your hands against the sides of the door frame.

Stay there for a minute or two pressing as hard as you can.

When you step away from the door you will find that your arms appear to float upwards of their own accord.

It's weird!

Hand Stand

Bend down and place one hand on the floor. Lift one of your legs slightly as if you are about to perform a one-handed hand stand. But before you go any further you stand up and say to a friend 'I can stand on one hand. Can you?'

Unless your friend is very athletic – or a show off – he or she will have to say 'No.'

As soon as your friend replies you say: 'I can.' You then place one hand on the floor and stand on it!

6 Play the Game

All you need for these games is yourself – and a few friends to play with. Provided, of course, that they are game to play!

Bend Over – and Run

It is always good fun to take part in a running race with your friends. But races can be even more fun if you adopt some unusual body position first.

In this version all you have to do is bend over and hold your ankles. Now have a race to a set point with your friends.

People who let go of their ankles or fall over have to go back to the start line and try again.

BODY FACT

The average human nose can distinguish some 4000 different scents, but someone who has a really sensitive nose can recognise up to 10,000 different odours.

Links

The players form themselves into pairs for this game. Each couple then link arms together so that they are back to back.

When the referee shouts 'Go' each pair runs from the start to the finishing line. The first pair to pass the finish line wins the race.

Any couple that unlink arms or fall over have to run back to the beginning and start again.

Leap Frog Race

Although this is a very old game it is still great fun to play.

Divide your friends up into teams of two people. The first person in the team bends down and grasps his knees (or lower down his legs if he is really fit).

The second person runs up to the first, places her hands on his back and uses them as a support and a lift as she jumps over him.

As soon as she lands the second person bends down and the first one then leaps over her.

This action is continued until both of them pass the finish line. The first team of two leap froggers to cross the line wins the race.

The Camel Train

This is not really a game. Neither is it a stunt or a trick. It is somewhere between the two. Sounds confusing, doesn't it!

It is fairly easy to understand but not so easy to do. Sounds even more confusing!

Gather together as many friends as you can and try this.

Each person bends down and holds the ankles of the person in front. The person at the front of the line is the only person who does not do this. 'Why is that?' you may ask. The answer is simple – there is no-one in front to hold on to!

So far, so good.

Now all you have to do is to see how far you can walk or run in this position before you all collapse into an untidy heap!

BODY FACT

In one minute an adult breathes in about six litres of air although only about four litres actually reach the part of the lungs where oxygen is taken from it.

Through the Arms

Clasp your hands together with your arms held straight out in front of you.

Now bring your hands down (keeping them clasped) and step through the loop formed by your arms.

Once your hands are behind your knees you can unclasp your hands. Bring your hands to the front of your body and clasp them together again. You can now repeat the whole procedure.

You should be able to do this without too much trouble. But let us now take it one step further.

Get several of your friends to have a race using only this method of moving forward. You now have a simple game that is a great deal of fun. The first person to cover a pre–determined distance is of course the winner.

It could be a good idea to have a referee for the race just in case anyone cheats. It just depends on how much you can trust your friends!

Wheelbarrows

Wheelbarrows are usually made of metal, plastic or wood. But to make the wheelbarrow used in this game all you need is two people.

To form the wheelbarrow one person lies face down on the ground. The second person stands near the feet of the first and takes one of his ankles in each hand. As the ankles are lifted the first person raises himself up on his hands.

It is now possible to move forward – the person who is standing walking normally and the other person walking on his hands.

If you can get enough people you can all pair up to form wheelbarrows and you can race against one another. As it is not unusual for the wheelbarrows to collapse such races can be quite hilarious.

BODY FACTS

A woman's heart beats faster than a man's.

Arm Wrestling

This is a game that tests the strength of one person against that of another.

The two players sit on opposite sides of a table. It is important that the table is high enough for the two players to rest their elbows on it without any discomfort. It should also be narrow enough to allow them to clasp their hands together as shown in the picture.

And now the battle is on. Each player pushes against his opponent's hand and tries to force it over and down to touch the table top. The first one to do so is the winner.

Shake Hands

This is another game of strength for two players.

The two opponents face each other and place right feet forward. They hold hands as if shaking hands.

Each player now tries to pull the other off balance. The first player to move his right foot is the loser.

Hop It

This is similar to the last game but here each player holds his or her left ankle with the left hand.

Once again the object of the game is to pull the other person off balance. The first one to let go of the ankle or the first one to fall to the ground is the loser.

BODY FACT

Your left lung is smaller than your right lung. There is an amazingly simple reason for this. It is to allow enough room for your heart.

Simon Says

In this game one person is first selected as the leader. She faces the other players and tells them to do various things – like raising both arms, standing on one leg, tapping the head, raising the left arm and so on.

If, before each order, the leader says 'Simon says' the players must carry out the action. If she does not say 'Simon says' but merely gives the order the players must not move.

So, if the leader says: 'Simon says do this' the players must obey.

But if she says: 'Do this' – the players must not move.

If a player makes a mistake then he or she is out of the game.

The last remaining player is the winner of that game and becomes the leader for the next game.

There are at least two ways in which the leader can try to confuse the players:

1. She can call out the commands as quickly as possible.
2. She can do several similar actions in quick succession and then suddenly change to something completely different. With a bit of luck several of the players will do the previous movement and so will be out of the game.

BODY FACT

A human hair is so strong it can support a weight of up to 3kg.

Do This, Do That

This is similar to the last game.

When the leader says 'Do this' the players must follow the action.

If the leader says 'Do that' the players have to remain still.

As in the previous game any person who does not follow the action after the instruction 'Do this', or who does the action after the words 'Do that' is out of the game.

The last player to remain in the game becomes the leader for the next game.

Limbo

This is a game based on a popular dance of the West Indies.

You will need a long pole, or a broom and two people to hold it gently.

Players then take it in turns to lean backwards and 'walk' under the pole. They are not allowed to touch the pole, nor to touch the floor with their hands.

At first this is fairly easy to do as the pole is held quite high. But after the players have gone under the pole the two holders lower it slightly.

The players then try again. Anyone who touches the pole, puts their hands to floor or falls over is out.

After each round the pole is lowered and only those players who get under it successfully are allowed to enter the next round. The winner is the person who can 'walk' under the pole at the lowest height.

BODY FACT

A human heart beats about 42 million times a year.

Freeze!

For this game you need at least four people but it is much better if you can get more than four to play.

One person is selected as the catcher and has to stand with his or her back to the other players who are lined up a short distance away.

As soon as the catcher's back is turned the other players move forward. At any time the catcher can turn round, and all the other players must 'freeze' on the spot. They must suddenly become like statues – perfectly still.

If, on turning round, the catcher sees anyone moving, that person is out of the game. The catcher turns back again and the players move forward – until the catcher turns round again.

The winner is the first player who can get right up to the catcher and touch him or her without the catcher having seen that player moving at any point. The winner becomes the catcher for the next game.

A catcher who eliminates all the players before anyone reaches him or her remains as catcher for the next game.

If you're an eager Beaver reader, perhaps you ought to try some more of our exciting titles. They are available in bookshops or they can be ordered directly from us. Just complete the form below and enclose the right amount of money and the books will be sent to you at home.

THE BEAVER BOOK OF MAGIC	Gyles Brandreth	95p	☐
MR ENIGMA'S CODE MYSTERIES	Tim Healey	95p	☐
THE HORROR'S HANDBOOK	Eric Kenneway	95p	☐
THE RUBBER BAND BOOK	Eric Kenneway	£1.00	☐
CAN PLANTS TALK?	Ralph Levinson	£1.00	☐
HOW TO MAKE SQUARE EGGS	Paul Temple and Ralph Levinson	£1.00	☐
THE BEAVER BOOK OF FOOTBALL	Tom Tully	60p	☐
AN A-Z OF MONSTERS	Ian Woodward	95p	☐
THE BEAVER HOLIDAY QUIZ	Robin May	85p	☐
THE BEAVER BOOK OF BRAIN TICKLERS	Charles Booth Jones	85p	☐
THE BEAVER BOOK OF TONGUE TWISTERS	Janet Rogers	80p	☐

And if you would like to hear more about Beaver Books, and find out all the latest news, don't forget the BEAVER BULLETIN. If you just send a stamped self-addressed envelope to Beaver Books, 17-21 Conway Street, LONDON W1P 6JD, we will send you one.

If you would like to order books, please send this form, and the money due to:

HAMLYN PAPERBACK CASH SALES, PO BOX 11, FALMOUTH, CORNWALL, TR10 9EN.

Send a cheque or postal order, and don't forget to include postage at the following rates: UK: 45p for the first book, 20p for second, 14p thereafter to a maximum of £1.63; BFPO and Eire: 45p for first book, 20p for second, 14p per copy for next 7 books, 8p per book thereafter; Overseas: 75p for first book, 21p thereafter.

NAME...

ADDRESS...

....

PLEASE PRINT CLEARLY

STRANGERS IN THE HOUSE

Joan Lingard

Calum resents his mother remarrying. He doesn't want to move to a flat in Edinburgh with a new father and a thirteen-year-old step-sister. Stella, too, dreads the new marriage. Used to living alone with her father, she loathes the idea of sharing their small flat with Willa, the silent Calum and his irrepressible young sister, Betsy. Stella's and Calum's struggles to adapt to a new life while trying to cope with all the problems of growing up are related with great insight and poignancy, in a book which will be enjoyed by all older readers.

PONIES IN THE FOREST

Christine Pullein-Thompson

Rosie, Clara and Andy help their parents run the Park Farm animal centre. Thinking they need extra help, their father recruits Silas, a boy from the local remand home, to help with the gardening. Silas is quiet and hard-working, but the children don't trust him, even though he is good with the animals, especially the horses. And then something so terrible happens they can hardly bear it, and it seems as if Silas has appeared in his true colours at last. Or has he? This exciting adventure story is a sequel to PONIES IN THE PARK and will be enjoyed by all animal lovers.

BLACK BEAUTY'S FAMILY 1

Diana and Christine Pullein-Thompson

Here are two stories about Black Beauty's relations. Black Romany, three generations before Black Beauty, was a well-bred horse who lived at Belvoir Castle. He hunted with Prince Albert and had lots of exciting adventures trekking across England. Blossom, six generations later, was not so lucky. The product of an unfortunate alliance, she had a life of drudgery working as a cart-horse, and her future seemed bleak until, out of the blue, came unexpected success.

PONIES IN THE PARK

Christine Pullein-Thompson

When Andy, Rosie, Clara and their mother are left Park Farm by an elderly uncle, Rosie thinks her dreams have come true. They can live in the country, and have ponies, and learn to ride! But the farm has to pay its way, and their efforts to turn it into an animal centre, with different breeds of ponies and other tourist attractions, are fraught with all kinds of problems. Somehow they must make it work, but can they do it in time? All animal lovers will thoroughly enjoy this exciting adventure story.